DEMCO

LIGHTNING BOLT BOOKS™

What Can You Do with MONEY?

Earning, Spending, and Saving

Jennifer S. Larson

Lerner Publications Company
Minneapolis

For Isaiah

Lerner Publications Company
A division of Lerner Publishing Group, Inc.
241 First Avenue North
Minneapolis, MN 55401 U.S.A.

Website address: www.lernerbooks.com

Library of Congress Cataloging-in-Publication Data

Larson, Jennifer S., 1967–
    What can you do with money?: earning, spending, and saving / by Jennifer S. Larson.
       p.   cm. — (Lightning bolt books™—Exploring economics)
    Includes index.
    ISBN 978-0-7613-3910-6 (lib. bdg. : alk. paper)
    1. Wages—Juvenile literature. 2. Income—Juvenile literature. 3. Consumption (Economics)—
    Juvenile literature. I. Title.
    HD4909.L25 2010
    331.2′1—dc22   2009027468

Manufactured in the United States of America
1 — BP — 12/15/09

Contents

Earning Money

Have you ever sold lemonade or cookies? Did you make some money?

When someone works at a paid job, he or she earns money.

Goods and Services

People use their income to buy goods and services. Goods are the things we eat, wear, and use.
A good is something you can touch.

A cookie is a good.

Services are work done by people for others.

Selling cookies to someone is a service.

Do you like to make things?
When you make something,
you create a good.

This boy made a
sea life scene.

Many people have jobs making goods.

These people are painting pottery. Pottery is a good.

Do you like to help other people? When you do something for someone else, that's a service.

Babysitting is a service.

Many people have jobs
providing a service.
Your teacher provides a
service—teaching you!

Many Kinds of Jobs

How many workers does it take to make a carton of strawberries? A lot! Farmers grow the strawberries.

Workers pick the strawberries. Then train and truck drivers deliver the fruit to a factory.

Factory workers sort the strawberries. Next, they put them in packages. Grocery store workers put the packages on display in the store.

14

AGRUP.PROD. DE LEPE

A checkout clerk sells the
strawberries to your family.
All of these workers
earn wages.

People don't always earn money for their work.

Your mom or dad provides goods and services at home.

Dinner is a good.
Washing the dishes
is a service!

Making Choices

Each family chooses how to use its income. First, a family spends money on the goods and services it needs. Food is a good we need.

This woman is making a budget. A budget helps a family figure out how to use its income.

Care from a doctor is a service we need.

Is there any money left after the family pays for its needs? If so, the family might decide to donate money. That means they give money to someone else who needs it.

The family might also choose to save some money. You can save money in a piggy bank or a jar. A bank is another place to save your money.

Spending Money

A family could decide to spend their extra money on something they want. A ski trip is a want. A kitchen table is a want. They may have to choose between the vacation and the table.

This family is buying a new bed.

We see things to buy almost everywhere. We can buy toys, an apple, or a ride on a roller coaster. How do we decide?

Think carefully about your choices. Is there something you'd like to buy? Is it worth spending your money on? Or should you save your money?

Would you buy this giraffe? Or would you save to buy a different toy?

If you save, you might be able to buy something better later on. You can make a list of what you'd like!

Some kids get an allowance. Do you?

An allowance is money that adults in some families regularly give to the kids.

Or maybe you earn wages doing chores for a neighbor. What will you do with your money?

Wants and Needs

Look at the pictures below. Which ones are needs? Which ones are wants? Write your answers on a separate sheet of paper.

Save or Spend?

You just got ten dollars for your birthday! Should you save it or buy a toy? Make a list. What are some good reasons for saving? For spending? Here is a sample list to get you started.

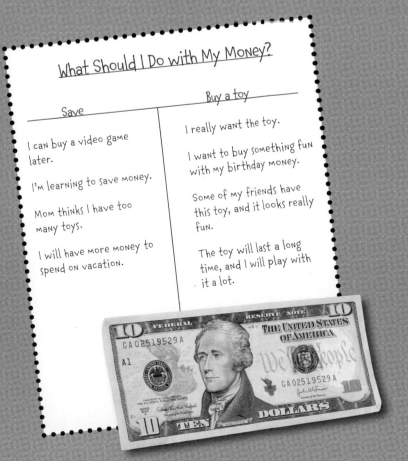

What Should I Do with My Money?

Save	Buy a toy
I can buy a video game later.	I really want the toy.
I'm learning to save money.	I want to buy something fun with my birthday money.
Mom thinks I have too many toys.	Some of my friends have this toy, and it looks really fun.
I will have more money to spend on vacation.	The toy will last a long time, and I will play with it a lot.

Glossary

allowance: money that adults in some families regularly give to the kids

donate: to give money to someone who needs it

earn: to get money for work done

good: a thing you can touch that can be bought and sold

income: money a person earns or receives

need: goods and services people must have to live

save: to keep money for later

service: work done by people for others

wages: money a person makes for working at a job

want: goods and services people do not need to live

Further Reading

Bair, Sheila. *Isabel's Car Wash.* Morton Grove, IL: Albert Whitman & Company, 2008.

Enchanted Learning: Budget http://www.enchantedlearning.com/economics/budget

Hill, Mary. *Spending and Saving.* New York: Children's Press, 2005.

Larson, Jennifer S. *Do I Need It? Or Do I Want It?: Making Budget Choices.* Minneapolis: Lerner Publications Company, 2010.

Nelson, Robin. *What Do We Buy?: A Look at Goods and Services.* Minneapolis: Lerner Publications Company, 2010.

Index

Photo Acknowledgments

The images in this book are used with the permission of: © Todd Strand/Independent Picture Service, pp. 2, 4, 7, 10; © iStockphoto.com/redmal, p. 5; © iStockphoto.com/Kativ, p. 6; © iStockphoto.com/Donna Coleman, p. 8; © Poppy Betty/CORBIS, p. 9; Yellow Dog Production/Digital Vision/Getty Images. P 11; © Karen Kasmauski/CORBIS, p. 12; © Ed Kashi/CORBIS, p. 13; © Chris Sattlberger/The Image Bank/Getty Images, p. 14; © Jack Hollingsworth/Photodisc/Getty Images, p. 15; © Pascal BRONZE/ONOKY/Getty Images, p. 16; © Gary John Norman/The Image Bank/Getty Images, p. 17; ©Cathy Yeulet/Glowimages.com, p. 18; © Bambu Productions/Iconica/Getty Images, p. 19; © Christopher Griffin/StockphotoPro.com, p. 20; © David Fischer/Photographers Chioce RF/Getty Images, p. 21; © iStockphoto.com/kristian sekulic, p. 22; Reflexstock/ © Juice Images, p. 23; Reflexstock/Corbis RF/ © Tim Pannell, p. 24; © Julie Caruso, p. 25; © Jacobs Stock Photography/Digital Vision/Getty Images, p. 26; © Julie Caruso/Independent Picture Service, p. 27; © iStockphoto.com/Mark Evans, p. 28 (robot); © iStockphoto.com/Photographer, p. 28 (skateboard); © iStockphoto.com/redmonkey8, p. 28 (chocolate bar); © matka Waraitka/Shutterstock Images, p. 28 (shoes); © Guido Oesterlein/Shutterstock Images, p. 28 (apple); © Jose AS Reyes/Shutterstock Images, p. 28 (bed); © Brie Cohen/Independent Picture Service, p. 29; © iStockphoto.com/Edyta Pawtowska, p. 30, © iStockphoto.com/Nicky Gordon, p. 31.

Front cover: © Todd Strand/Independent Picture Service.